A Red Witch, Every Which Way

hysterical boooks
2016

A Red Witch, Every Which Way

Juliet Cook
&
j|j hastain

Hysterical Boooks
2016

Copyright © Juliet Cook and j/j hastain 2016
All rights reserved under
International and Pan-American Copyright Conventions.

No portion of this book may be reproduced in any form without the written permission of the publisher, except by a reviewer, who may quote brief passages in connection with a review for a magazine or newspaper.

Cover Image: Carabella Sands

Design, production: Jay Snodgrass
Library of Congress Cataloging-in-Publication Data
A Red Witch, Every Which Way
by Juliet Cook and j/j hastain — First Edition
ISBN — 978-0-940821-04-0
Library of Congress Cataloging Card Number — 2016930074

HYSTERICAL BOOKS
1506 Wekewa Nene • Tallahassee, Florida 32301
Email: hystericalbooks@gmail.com

Published in the United States by Hysterical Books
Tallahassee, Florida • First Edition, 2016

~Juliet Cook would like to dedicate this book to j/j hastain
&
~j/j hastain would like to dedicate this book to Juliet Cook

The mutated conjoined twins:
one can fly and one can swim.
Do you take turns throwing them
up and down or tear them apart?
Do you rip them into a multitude of pieces?
No matter what, this will be bloody.

contents

Act 1
The Secret Carnage Hidden in a Cuckoo Clock

Chords   13
What Do You Desire For This Valentine's Day?   14
Red Rocks Inside My Froth-A-Goth   15
Fruit Shaped   17
Inside Out Again   19
The Pumpkin Gut Fur of the Fairy Tale   20
Pre-Bacon   22
Chicken Feed   24
Goop   26
Inside Out Entangled Twine   28
Elated Excavation   30
Cuckoo Loincloth   31
Crooked Clock Work   33
The Secret Carnage of Female Fairies While They Wait in Women's Rooms   34
Fugitive Dive   36
Paradoxical Flight   38
Paradoxical Dive Back Down   40
Animal Mutation   42

Act 2
The Mutated Conjoined Twins

Access Achieved Then Denied   45
Instead of the Doctor   46
Another Tainted Device   47
A Tiny Unbroken Snow Flower Stuck Inside   49
Clawing At The Confessional   51
Blood Bath Through Water Balloons   52
It's A Bird... It's A Plane... It's...   54
No More Promises   56

Misshapen Mouths   57
Disjunction From an Open-Ended Instrument   60
She   61
New Superhero   62
Testing   63
Below Water Whores Bemoan   64
Defenestration Below Ground   67
Porous   69
Anti-Mold Momentum   70
Wonderland or Wanderlust   72
Banshees   74

Act 3
An Underworld's Spring Filled With Questions

Go Ahead and Rip Off These Witch Tits And See What Happens Next   79
A Multitude of Red Ring Fingers   80
Clots Push Over the Edge 84
Blood Red Cloudbursts   86
Broken Burial   87
Disinfectant or Douche?   89
The Healing Potion Explodes   90
Incinerated Psalms of Blood   91
Torso Chamber Orchestra   94
Grave Contortionism   97
Conjured Talisman   99
Create Your Own Rise and Fall 101
Oh Black Swan Pie Seasoned and Sliced   104

Juliet and j/j Interview Each Other

Acknowledgements: 126
Bios: 127

A Red Witch, Every Which Way

Act 1

The Secret Carnage hidden in a Cuckoo Clock

Chords

You reach your hand into your empty body and pull
out an entire, frothing cornucopia of pink
doll eyes, writhing tongues, flesh and glass.

An ethics that slithers and contorts: bloody cherry
baby mouth,
girls milk,
wrists, black throat cake.

Blowfish bursts your lagoon.
A reason to pull a rune, to trust a true color.
The sun might express itself by accepting
you into its blue hour. Cloudbursts of scarred art
iculation reshaped to tiny stars, shapely
retention tar smeared with a skinless hand
over a line. A bardo. How to move down
into discord or swoon up into a lullaby
or both?

What Do You Desire for This Valentine's Day?

Maybe an exacto knife slice between one of these
sweet ribs to slip in a secret letter. A dripping wet
new kind of eye candy. A new heart machine
painted with aorta gore art. Inside that vertebra,
mutant locusts sing and sway, wrapped in macabre
cobweb dresses. Semi-translucent layers of ticking,
netting, birdcage wires and bones, then cysts flooding.

Flooding over with hoardable contents. The ducts
and catacombs as spillways by which contour chemicals
reach us, offer us a drip of painted flank as aperitif
or offer us adrip, period. The waxing
of fluids so like a moon of conduits
that will slowly redden and moan
their own sonorous body language.

I need to hear what is being said below me.
I need the red immediacy
as the soil begins seeping.
Anywhere blood is present,
war also is. Or birth, chosen
death, pro-evacuation. Our seeds
to be pulled out of standard ground
and transplanted however we choose.

Red Rocks Inside My Froth-A-Goth

Foliage,
the rawest riff raff
on an early morning when the night is
still present.

You
and your strange
ransack of leaves
that are attached

to something
unattached.

We
must be ratcheting our way
through a Buddhist
text on attachment.

We talk about what isn't in order
to look at what is.

Outside the garden,
the cuckoo clock turns
into a cocoon,
dirty and stuck.

Strap it on,
peel it off,
you know you want to rotate
the layers.

With subliminal layers,
we know we want to sublimate ourselves

into a new fold and then
work our way out of it again.

We always return to the in and
then the out.
Sexualization of animations
leading the way towards

animated mutations
inside a mixed drink.

Fruit Shaped

A drip of oil paint inside each mug,
now chug it.

Churn a weather system
around the sun until you
recognize and can thereby name it
captive.

Tiny raptors inside the glass
will grow, newly created
limbs,

but that doesn't mean wing spans
can fly unless they turn
paranormal.

Panorama perspective: persimmons

being penetrated by soft
greens.

Gauges gabbing away at
midnight.

Witches brewing
a mug from a coffin
with a heart shaped eel inside.

Remember that child's
party game

where you took turns
bobbing for apples? Or where
you de-virginated the
long-lasting plum,
then placed it inside
the freezer
until it burned.

Inside Out Again

Like a bee moth with bloody honeycomb lips.
Whose mouth will you sting next?
Whose mouth will become your own
next sticky chrysalis space?

Behemoth please don't
lose yourself while you are busy
trying to find yourself.
Don't treat your stingers
like they're tectonic plates.

You're not the whole surface of the earth.
You hover buzz above the mainstream,
but why try to create a new ovicide?
Are you attempting to kill
your own pattern again?

When will you help yourself
understand not every protrusion turns
into a broken down strand of tainted
confidence in the hyoid coincidence?

Are you too busy chiding biology to notice
your disembodiment tear apart like
flayed digits? You used to be pretty
as a snap dragon until you snapped,

and repeatedly ripped yourself
into too many different pieces.

The Pumpkin Gut Fur of the Fairy Tale

Immeasurable mass
not a flag: a note
though. When the soft spot
you happened
to make in the sandstone
side
offers a pocket
place
your sodden projections
your discordant contours
heading close to the circle
shaped edges of quicksand.

Shaggy carpet
on which we repent
lend more than a hand
for what has been done to
land animals,
snakes that can't slither anymore

except inside their own heads,
because something tore it out
of them of the pumpkin
and ate it.
Yes I'm talking out of the box pumpkin guts
and an off with their heads
fairy tale nightmare
fused with stale pie crust
and hissing pie holes,
a nightmare felt not at night
but while
Cinderella is burning

cinders
and a wakeful aching
to release another snake, a sizzle
of pink and grey
mating calls.

Pre-Bacon

Pig Latin is spoken
by a fetal pig in a jar,
aimed to create a peculiar
assortment of jewels
that turn into liquid cement

and then
the fetal pig breaks itself
out of the jar,
starts dancing
through the whole room,
smelling it up
with formaldehyde.

In the back room,
special unguents
are prepared.
The new sound track
when the jar and the pig
are thrown onto
the literal
cement.

In other words: hey diddle diddle
the cat in the fiddle
the cow jumped over the tomb
the little pig snorted
peed on the sacred site
and stuck its own pig tail
into a blender

to create a new defibrillator
one two three
zap and

glee!

The little piggy's mother is now
riding bareback
in the middle
of another broken heart.

Chicken Feed

1.

You might
bulk me up
on gingerbread.

You know
you can't wait to dive in
to hot flesh.

You know where
to find me,
how to bind me
into the latest
shallow halo.

Turn on
the oven.

2.

Turn me over
and say something reductive
of me.

Impacting and empowering
you.

Act like every other aggressor
with your chin hair and your ugliness
inside.

Baba Yaga
what will it take for you
to soften?

Wet the dirty mud
off those giant chicken legs
and watch what happens
inside this house.

Goop

Again I awoke from this dream.

You were grossed out
by my words
then suddenly changed
your mind. You wanted to take
a chance,
to lie
down
surrounded
by shit.

You wanted to get stuck
in it
your hair
ripped out,
watch it grow

wet soil
transplants. Hair a navigational
comrade. The words
were boulders
mossy pits, wounds.
The words were mutating
crows, cawing through
every socket,
every crawlspace.

With new sounds,
the words were extensions
the place where the bridge is

beginning
to separate
the loam foams
and spurts out
a tiny volcano

flipped so the cone tip
is at the bottom. It is leaking. Honey,
lay down here beside me. I think
it is time to dream again.

Inside Out Entangled Twine

Half the size of a big banana
but sweet as hell and high
the spine covered
my winding mind
all of time
dispersing

Identity lines
are brine
possibly needed
possibly not

I want your
twisted branches
I am
misshapen pine needles
phallus
and scree

I am another
emergence by ancient
wailing ghoul
a talus
a tone

I am a roaming
rune
with a talisman
inside me

How many times
will I have to beg you
don't clear cut
this aromatic
dome

Elated Excavation

I'm an incomparable mess with exaggerated streaks.
How do I narrow this down? During weeks
of drought--during weeks
of downpour--weeks upon weeks of
inauguration of weakness. Why is my flesh
made like this? Is it made for this? I didn't
sign up but it might be time
to excavate and rearrange the flock.

Here's my latest signature. I am glowing the more and more
sheep I let into this
dream state.
Sheep aren't only a bridge, aren't only
what to count in order
to get somewhere. When the moon is just right,
these sheep trigger out ectoplasm,

lots of different colors and
shapes, too many to count
unless we create a whole
different sort of order
reordering the borders while
wise men dream of dust bunnies
and other happenstance. Revamp
the squiggle dusters into ecstatic
elation, frenetic deviation
from the fur
or devotional pledges ensuring
the fur.

Fury dangling on the edge,
purring at you to count
yourself in

Cuckoo Loincloth

Why Lancelot? She asked
her other self
the one in the oculus.

Why not a lion-sized lark
a lionized loincloth
chewing this month's blood

in order to create sparkles
of bewitching lioness drips
as the creature learns to fly.

When the full moon
is acting full out
in attempt at fulfilling

will you drink it
or will you pull out
the flying machete

and try to hit that moon
down? Because why try?
Why attempt flight?

It's like the spasm of a clock
made out of milkweed
that might suddenly turn cuckoo

and then drip down thighs
and crawl out the door
again. Screech as the glass
breaks. Great gallbladder
gonads in a rococo arrangement
with lip gloss on top.

Crooked Clock Work

This pumpkin is crooked.
I mean, maybe this pumpkin doesn't fall
all that far from the tree, but
it falls down even more crookedly,
then any other branch you'll ever see.

And who built this tree?
Did they say it was stuck
in one place? You are going to cook
the colors looking for
cuckoo birds from within.

They aren't from the grandfather clock.
Grandpa's cock didn't do anyone much
good. A bird bathing in a frumpy shirt,
a goofy mood,
a grumpy groom.

An overused birdbath moon
repeatedly followed by clichéd bedtime
stories in which you know who was always on top (grandpa)
even though he weighed 300 pounds more than you.

He didn't seem to have a problem crashing on top of you
even if he fell asleep, crushed your bones, and snored so
loud your ears would have broken too if you didn't
make them turn into small pumpkin clocks.

The Secret Carnage of Female Fairies While They Wait in Women's Rooms

1.

These dead birds in their infant bloat stages,
managed to turn themselves
into tiny incubus.

If another evil creature
could lift them
and fly them into a sleeping woman's

bedroom, the dream state
invasion might create
new, twisted feathers.

The reaming invasion might turn
small tirades into long tunes.

More and more we concern
ourselves with the sounds of songs unable to be
sung, unable to be flung across

the room into the half-broken mirror
unless we want it to crack again. Yet,
my dear, if we travel to the city tonight

and bring exactly three ripe peaches
along in your purse, I strongly suspect
when we extract them, we will get to watch

at least one of them turn
into a half-broken egg
that once cracked open drips bright red.

2.

More and more we corner
ourselves under beds, pressed
against walls and listen to it

drip even more droplets
of dark red dredge.
Surprised and not surprised we

pull the pistils, the stamens,
the hot little steam engines
outside of contorted yolks.

Our thighs are pounding,
counting down the moments

before the firecrackers
unleash yet another
red birdbath. In other words,

we push origin from its frame,
a dreamtime, but within a broken
cuckoo clock. A red snake pops out

of another bloody hole. Are our eyes
mutant charmers? Are our brains
more dream state orbs, bound to

continue dripping down nightmare tracks?

Fugitive Dive

Strong alternating tides
fling flagella
all the way up
to the top of the tree lines

then branches break and we
mis-perceive this to be
a result
of added weight.

Really it was a result
of the dialogue we had
about angels overtaking
an antique syringe
and the torn space, absorbing
the tidal pool fluids.

A wedged interface
is discharging into sockets
filled with bloody
body parts
fused with filo dough.

Rotating around glands,
dripping mutant strands.
Brightening all of that bleached hair.

We're leading the way up towards
the bleachers, then hurling down
nosebleeds onto the cheerleaders.

Then they finally exit the gym,
carrying small strobe lights.
They climb all the way up
to the top of the silo to meet us.

We come together
to dance
our way back inside.

Paradoxical Flight

A new rib cage
bursts out bright
eye-colored marbles
oil catching the light

as something tangible
hard pressed.
I mention the mighty
density
of letting go of delight

when a road kill
cat
black
silk cradles a
hyper notch
broken down
purring
crotch panel
rotting neural
blotch

an aural
round path
so partial
pussy extract
carefully oozing
from new particles

networks
jet stream
proving

an either or
model
incoherent
the bed holds
the bed folds
and parallel shifts
re-grow new propellers

living
an order in
order
wonder
cylindrical calendar
call

nine lives of
underwater propulsion
and new birth

before the season shifts
and too much
mirth
gathers
in the crevice
between thighs

then blood drenched ether explodes
sky high.

Paradoxical Dive Back Down

Christen by chrism
chasing unattainable
chastity. Graft a suit
to assist you with the state
of your wrists.

Drizzling splayed fluff
or is it blood combined with moon silver?

They can tell you you're splatter painting down
the steeples but you're creating your own
red-toned ventricles
your own everlasting tome.

Who knew the body could be
so much? Who will hold
the splayed sides of the casket
for your next body (p)art?

Me myself and I?
Charm school/chasm/eyeballs
burst out and fly
off the rails.

Were guardrails
supposed to keep things
on the road? Or be bent
as ramps to shoot
moving amples
up like chutes. We
are making our way toward
flight and it keeps making us

ricochet out spires that shoot
spores instead of bullets: a relief
a reason to keep
on in the name of Gaia

Whether in fracture
or in frith how do we contain
our oscillating umbilicus
and what if
he or she
did in fact
jump off,
leap?

Into the boiling sea,
every bit of skin sizzling
collarbones steaming
voice box glinting out
undulating sting rays
wrapped around mons
venus heat, (non)human meat
sparkling waves of killer teeth.

Paradise found.

Animal Mutation

Splayed and simmering
like hot snow spiked my drink.

I was mooing on the sidelines.
Had I become

a Molotov cocktail shaped like a horse
or a Cockatoo hiding under glass?

Help. I can't figure out how to
truncate myself before I explode.

Help. Am I helping myself into a heap
wishing
for a lover to emerge from popped
balloons
valves
baby calves

jerking around
under broken umbrellas,

turning into misshapen
cattle prods,

not the right size
to stick inside
a body bag.

Act 2
The Mutated Conjoined Twins

Access Achieved Then Denied

Reconstructed glitter cavern
with explosive devices inside

a cave in a mouth
unexpected

Some thought they were extinct,
but some new the strange truth –
part of that
trilobite
was going
to come back to life
as a twin

thinning
ossein to massage

scrim by which to scry
mutant shrapnel made

of diabolical kinship not sure
how we got from making to
razing but somehow we have
wagered our way
into wagging
beneath a cloak
under our conjoined parts

like limbs of old growth trees
how did we get so entangled?

enshrined axis
until someone gets the ax.

Instead of the Doctor

Conjoined at the slit
and so
the mortician
gets out
her scalpel.
Blades dissect

grass. An acerbic area
in May.
A mother at a mall
uses her tweezers to
protect and to serve,
but then the little vixen swerves

into the back room
of the toy store
and hides in between
the lines of microscopes.
They bend and sway
in the fan wind.

Is microorganism necrophilia
crawling around the ceiling
in between the light
and dark swirls? Is that little
girl soon to be extracted
by the experimental mortician?

Awaiting her latest turn,
and then fired
into a misshapen urn.

Another Tainted Device

I dropped you in
to the kiln
and then
ran for my life.

I had been meaning to
put you out
of your misery this way
for years, since you
were a toddler,
actually.

You kept on growing
bigger and bigger
boobs and cueing
laugh tracks
to stand in
for actual human emotion.

I had been hoping to
turn you into a real
boy. By that I mean
harnessed and kept
clean. No beard hair or scrotum
stretches but not a ken doll
either.

Talk about an abnormal moon dance
when that cock kept growing
bigger than your boobs,
bigger than any human

and then even bigger
than any cartoon character.

I mean what was I supposed to do?
I designed and constructed my own
one-of-a-kind giant kiln and then
managed to dance you across the room
in a contorted ballroom dance fashion,
in an overstretched out ballroom gown.

A form,
a liaison
a nutritive psychosis
leading closer to

a new explosion.

A Tiny Unbroken Snow Flower Stuck Inside

I accidentally burnt a branch
of
my family tree.

See, I was raised
Mormon. I wasn't raised
out of a womb

and then flung
onto a conveyor belt
or was I? I mean,

I am so much of the matter
from which I was born
but I am also
how I was reared.

Hence the need
to create my own
tourniquet
and rip it off when I choose.

Hence the need to cut
one of my own fingers
and reshape it into a bible
bookmark that drips through
some of the lines.

Another confession
for the trinity, for this uncanny
obsession with threes.

When I lift my finger to you, father
I am still flipping out
on the speed

of my never ending 666
paranoid streak.
One half a nun uniform.

One half a blood mask.
Two thirds a bloodied apron.
One whole caboodle

with an orchestra dripping down the walls
and staining the alter
ego

white as winter
snow
trapped in a snow blower.

Clawing At The Confessional

Shove a donation into another envelope
to swallow our mess.

Tithe a depth into a shallow-
push. Shudder pump my arms
into giant figurines.

Saint statue turns
into toy. Box-
elder stability

yearns for torn pages
in a series of open books.

Book marks rip
into extra sharp razor wire
encircling the crevasses.

Rest below this dripping
alter piece.

Confess your sins
as something you thought of
in too-thin of a philosophical frame.

Confess your sins
and admit you are
in need of love now.

Too bad
you don't believe
in love
anymore.

Blood Bath Through Water Balloons

The land began to tell us
it has its own identity by
way of rocking horses.

The teen was sick
of being called irreverent to which
he could only respond by saying
how irrelevant you all are.

Your horse feed is all the same color;
his is impalpable. Yet you call the shots.
You call it inedible, without even trying
to understand the possibilities
of visionary realignment.

You make demands with
your mouth shut.
Your eyes closed
when he tried
to show you his
long lace finger.

Too much shag rug
to see beneath.
Insects invading the base.
Basics evading the beast.
Ripping another nest egg
into buzzing pieces.

Another broken rocking horse leg
exploding up into
the sky.

Before landing in the
neighbors wide open
piñata.

It's A Bird... It's A Plane... It's...

The sparrow was cleaved
and placed upon two alters.

This was part of a new science
fair project based on alter ego,
but who created this? Which one of us?

You and me sister--I am talking
to you. The face in the mirror
blanches
like being called out on in class
when reading porn
behind
the open history book.

Not just any old porn.
Porn involving animals
cut in half.

But aren't we all cut
into multiple pieces
and different thought processes?

The way we see it,
this pornographic imagery
is turning our contorted minds
into physical amalgamations
of horror and lust.

The love of unusual curiosities.
The taboo placards painted in blood.
It starts to rain. It shows us

it really is possible to rain animals.

In the idiom they say cats and dogs, but more often it is
a phantasmagoria of brutally halved birds
still singing.

Amputated atrocities
emerging from pitcher plants
and picturing new flight.

No More Promises

My voice is lacking pitch.
No safety net. I am a lackey: red with drips
from ripped
chairs. Is it lava or plasma
or a menstrual blood hole
in the wall.

He turns his head up
toward me
from where he
has just hid it beneath
his underground
spot: chair is charred.

He wants to create his own paint colors.
No red allowed, none of my words.
He tells me I have bad taste
in color and music. "No more words you're
telling me you love me
while you're looking away."

He tells me he'd punch me in the face
if he didn't already know
I was going to bang my own head
into another red room without him.

Misshapen Mouths

1.
Convex to concave like a soft con
and pills forced inside her:
a slap stick comedy
involving an overdose of
hair and inertia.

"How can you overdose on inertia?"
Someone is shouting
from the black box,
trying to make themselves more
known. Then he starts throwing
pills in front of the camera.

Then he throws a wet bath towel
into a front row audience member's face.

Then the actress who was
overdosed starts convulsing
and throws up.

Take two. Let's try that again--
"Folks this will be an indefinite intermission."

2.
Behind the scenes, lace and laxative
feel the same on a body on a
portal siphoned into open mouths.

Just close your mouth already! You can't
shout with that discolored tongue
growing into a disco ball
crashing down from the ceiling.

You can't go forward
when all of the city's lights have turned
red. Are you real?

3.
A sunspot just descended
upon your garden. I thought
I heard something break. I broke
up with whatever is not
land. I ripped the trellises away
from the misshapen garden gnomes.

They started flying in every which way direction--
Home full of poison glands and biting tongues.

Disjunction From an Open-Ended Instrument

Like a non-poisonous caterpillar
stuck in a rat trap.
How dare they get out
another glue gun to stare,
take every bit of fuzz
off your bra from the dryer
and inspect for remnants
of your own desire.

Fold your body parts
into the proper position
and then stick them all
onto this giant web.
The scent of mold fills the room
and you will never understand
how they don't understand
how this smells sinister.

Well they call it daily life
and you can feel just how
wrong that is. You can feel
the poison welling up inside you,
contorting your genuine self
into a hiss, into a hissing cock
roach stock inside the valve
of a blaring trumpet.

She

Another swaddled slaughter.
You can't keep squirming
away from this scene.
Asphyxiation will turn
into ossification, put pressure
on the dream. Which one?

The twisted prop set
of trying to figure out if
this is an omen or your own
choice. Entreating for another
entry wound, more and more
extreme until the dream rips
a mermaid out of the water,

holds a machete up high
to the sun, then the double
fin returns. At half-light
many hours later, the sword
becomes an oyster catcher,
catching coal as the sun keeps

dying. Am I dying along with
the myth? Am I a discolored hag
fish trapped inside a vase?
A red witch, every which way
reminds us of the power of lights
to snag arteries, sudden fluctuations,
red disarray stuck inside a turntable.

Thrown down under water while still
trying to play my songs.

New Superhero

Pond scum will burst
out the eyes
once the eyes have been
revised into a film.

Watching a horror movie
and then fucking
the small holes between
frames. Spiraling

pinafores worn on
pin up girls. Ripped
wholeness
radiating curd.

Curdled blood
cells swaddling
clothes into
a new close up.

We are nude dolls with eyes
ripped out
and replaced
by repellent.

Testing

The opposite of coiffed,
slime molds attached to
disconnected pony tails,

gripping and dripping out
tainted protoplasm.
A ramp of spasms.

A reoccurring dream of rings
being taken off of fingers by
cutting the fingers off.

"Cupcake makeup glitter eye
shadow jar" filled with red signals
of nails and finger tips and ring tones.

Antennas inserted into
the wounds to sing out
a high-grade scream.

Below Water Whores Bemoan

1.
Cave
grave.

The sides of a face.

Subconscious scan
for any seam.

"I'm really not
picky, but my thigh-highs are
in full bloom
and nobody is
picking them!"

The weeds will soon
pop out of

the hole
in the bottom.

2.
Self conscious
waves hands

without wavering away.

All things conscious
but no longer swimming
(lobsters and sand dollars
stranded on the beach
and radioactive flaps abandoned).

Barter with me, my sweet
toxic sea.

When and how will my insides stop
popping out of my outsides?

When will I sink
down and drown?

3.
Shrinking and bobbing,
the buoy

extracts my pelvis
and turns it

into an underwater lap dance.

Defenestration Below Ground

A sticky floor
or a red drenched canvas.
A blur of something
from somebody
who doesn't exist
anymore.

How much more
skin do you think can be unpeeled
from this body before
it sails away for good
or evil?

Were we meant to be
ripped blow up dolls,
stuck in a cruise ship restroom
until the house cleaning
crew call the police
and have us admitted
for strip search scrutiny
of our few remaining
remnants of real flesh?

Covered with leeches
inside the holes.
Small placards each one
standardizing a mishap,

a misshapen bag stuffed
with pads and padded
masks. A factory
drenched with unclean
dream boats. How and when

does a dream actually become
full and clean? Will we have to
free it from literal
exit wounds?

Will we have to
wind it through
or throw it out
countless
windows
underwater?

Porous

A headless gray
angel
with a dark glitter intaglio.
A thoughtful message
inscribed. A figure
stands under

the full moon
wearing only
sandals. Black jelly sandals

lighting up the dark with pink
erupting heels. This planet's
constituents read through solar

flares, a folly
bypassing scarcity for
excess and scars.

Whole eclipses of stars.
Hole punches of stars
backstage. How do we
transform our broken legs
into a moving cataclysm?

First we must throw out
the crutches, watch albino toads turn
into red-eyed treasure seekers.

Blood-hued underwater
with new heads rising up
down
pour.

Anti-Mold Momentum

The phantom tries to mold me
into amber embryos
and as I gather pictures
along
the brink I break
cigarettes
little binkies
in a mouth unfinished.

Unfinished or not
the mold won't work.
I'll scream and break
glass
and then drink
what I broke out of.
It's been done before
chew the contents

then chew the form
as a way of making
both more content. Mysterious
risks. Glass grows stronger
and we pour our sea salt
into the glass cabinet.
Will it melt or crack or
break another mold,

release the latest specimen
racy and with crisp
momentum. A silo
a spillway being swallowed

in sallow halos will lead
towards self-created flying things.
It doesn't matter how far down
you throw me.

Even if I break again and again
I will re-grow, re-birth
create
new shapes
new directions.
Redefine this fodder.
Fold me out of the line,
not into it.

Wonderland or Wanderlust

Another broken clasp, hissing
on the upturned coast.
I did not mean to come this far
away without
something to warm
my hands

but the warnings, the grasping for
life
jackets, for jacked-off gasping

antibodies hidden in my hip flasks.
Three is more I
have three hips.

Swathe swaddle
swooning
inside this threesome of

nether region, tethered netherlands
tongue tied, speaking through
the eyes.

Wide
tokens
spying

gasping again
for another
breath of

three
pin-pricked lips
ruptured tips

render us as we wrestle
and our viscera
rips.

Banshees

whether lore or lie
I long for it in the tone of the lyre
does that make me
antiquated? I feel
past tense
even when I am dreaming
I feel
resistance to glacial
time

resistance to eye rolling
boredom. Rip it out
and swim in a blood bath
tidal pool

there are schools
in this scoop: fish, sperm,
mollusks floating
over a threshold
overt to them but
not mute.

have you ever heard the sound
of the leafy sea dragons
whispering inside your head
until they scream their way out?

ever neared the sound
of unexpected
squirming
as a form of steering
non-gloved hand
enters the backside of

utterly unique tubesnouts?

even though they're custom designed
and then birthed, sometimes
it's tricky to recall
exactly why and how
the armor, art, and fetish combine

into swimming paint, swimming horses,
swinging whips, swooning hips,
tongue jelly thigh bloomers
tonal dye

ever felt the sea
as a place without tides?
ever felt the ride
as an alignment
just shy of
tidal swarms

how could swans have
gotten in there
whole
wings
hatchlings
ripping their way out black holes,
replacing them with blue black hair
that can fly in and out
of the water world

submerge more linings
in curves

Act 3

An Underworld's Spring Filled With Questions

Go Ahead and Rip Off These Witch Tits And See What Happens Next

When the oracle first called
my name in an orgasmic
frenzy all my previous
frailty, my skin
frenzidly peeled off
and what's underneath
was bound to be
even bloodier.

I dreamed of giving birth
to a dripping fetal pig arboretum.

Intentional and unintentional abortions
were single-handedly responsible for
these blood-drenched gobstoppers
hacked out, then mummified,
then planted, then transplanted,
then re-planted into more
fetal pigs that can fly,
cackle like witches.

I needed these comrades so I no longer
had to cast spells alone.

A Multitude of Red Ring Fingers

1.
Chokecherries in the nest
or hang-gliders. If you're strapped

do you dive or let yourself dry? There are
many ways to try. Gather the hair
from the drain but before
garbage tracks it on the level of its
grains. A mirror fogs energy,
gathers drip drops. Marooned brain waves
with dark orange extract raises

an antler chandelier.
A rhythm
snags

your hearse full of tourniquets,
your mouth full of drive through
wine glasses oozing bile, then turning
not into something but
into through. It was not
until what surrounded changed
that more than one of

us
appeared.

2.
Then we dreamed our own nest
not filled with birds or bate but
blood. We could rest there all
morning
afternoon
evening
mowed and loaded with all kinds of fur.
Made up fur is no more faux than real fur
is ready to be
hot flax seed,
oil drenched with blood.

Red torrential downpours of
fetus wings. Ring finger
slough. Cut it off

and see
what is
inside
me:

this
trough of strange

transcendence.

3.
As the trees darken
no
redden.

As salivary glands
contort
and the limbs peek,

their crevasse peaks
anomalies that sting. "Good morning,"
then a cup of oolong curling under
the gaping knees, dripping ring

worms,
rigged torpor.
Sometimes the sinews
of the animal are the totem

burlesque with stage prop
blood spewing out
our vaginas.
The worms crawl in,
the worms crawl out

the crawlspace starts to fly
or cry.
The crawlspace is trying to stay alive,
energy
in and out,
circuitry.

The crawlspace is trying to cut off
that bracelet, to cut
off that brace,

to create our own
ember emblazoned embrace.

Clots Push Over the Edge

Trying to catch clots in glass jars.

A bottom leg cut off
in last night's dream.
I awaken with tremulous vibrations
vigorous iterations
after dreaming of amputated
legs running rampant
in a desert
I knew that I
was in a drought
with cast iron replacing the thighs
with no more liquid dripping out.

How will I create a bright new half
moon? How and why will
that moon will me
wet? I want
to be a cavern
open
unclenched
but right now
the dark pit
between
is pith
covered in
need of recovery.

Moon dance, moon dangled beads, I need
to bleed again.

I need ancient versions of me
not all of these exhausting weeds.

I need to rip out the weeds,
make hair for a marionette,
give her away and then
grow my own new hair.
Wing it out of this dry, dark spell.

Increase the decibel on complexity
of shamanist ringing
the marionette
drags and falls
a way of poking pins in
the rag doll
until it morphs

into a blood-dripping dessert.

Blood Red Cloudbursts

A week-long obsession with clouds
not unlike other humans
yet somehow more.
Cloudbursts through every keyhole
I peek into. Is this a dream?
Has my vision been whittled?

Or am I a visionary who must
figure out what the clouds stand for?
Rising up, sinking down, all the color
changes and the shapes like
strange rapes, reoccurring
rope lengths.

Ions and decay, a proliferation of
intravenous flying things, changing
wings, swelling and then exploding.
I am growing
unafraid of speaking.
Speech stenciling.

Each mouth a sharp
elongated portal.
Each direction once waxen,
a soft song encounter with strands
altering the stew, spewing out
new prototypes and quickly
revamping all light.

Broken Burial

Questing
longevity
as we peruse aisle after aisle of
unusual makeup
make me compose
a different
me.

Surrogate position
several
meat hooks hanging
from the edge.
Let them grow
their own meat.

Birth their own
dangling symphony.
Polyphonic ganglia.
Recombinant system. There are
good crimes. At least we thought
there were, but then

my so-called partner starts
eating them before they're ready.
It feels like every time I eat
it pulps out immediately,
it explodes itself inside me
instead of growing all the way.

I'm starting to hate my body.
The only way I can control it is if I starve,
stop planting, stop hanging
my art on my own hooked walls.

Maybe hating the hooks
is a better approach. Then I can keep
my body in the hidden
nook, but who
will I give my torn down hooks to
not to mention my broken down body?

Should I keep them all for myself,
split one more rib and bury it
in the dirt, find out what might grow?
Should I offer it to myself,
the bloody heap before
me a surprising deifying of me?
I am tired of doing all the work
myself. A long time ago I thought a lover
was real, but it was

just another corn husk doll
with blood sewn into
one socket ,with faux boldness
steering the rocket.

No wonder it keeps bursting into tears.

Disinfectant or Douche?

How do we engrave an orifice?

Burn a bible, a bundle,
an American flag.
Coagulate all the swag
down our throats and then
gag ourselves and spit it
down the drain and
grab the Lysol.

You know what we used to advertise
that Lysol for?

Cleaning off the stick of the plunger
after anal.

Prepare for ocular penetration
and spray paint a ventricle
with gasoline.

Blowtorch the entire panel,
turn the whole party scene
into burning whoopee cushions.

Quiet now: just experience that sound.

The Healing Potion Explodes

We were seeking
not
North
in other words the
womb
full of worms
the groom of
a returning blood flow
brimming with another line up
marooned brain waves.

Replicate life force
The void?
The new cave?

Is the place in which you are engaged
full to you? Or are you another never
ending cascade? Bright red, dark red.

One side a positive
healing
fetish violence.
One side a negative
stab wound
fantasy/reality.
Never ending hemorrhaging hemisphere. Never
ending lavish
light.

Incinerated Psalms of Blood

1.
Do you even know
what cremated body parts look like?

They might be bigger than you think.
They might be smaller than life,
but larger than death.

Visualize your own eyes growing
into red beet shapes,
one on each side.

2.
Envision the incision made
by unexpected incisors,
turning your roots
into shrapnel, then
setting them into flame.

Even if you never believed in hell,
you are now a burning carousel
dripping down.

Your afterlife will be mixed into
the eye holes of dead horses
and you will be praying
for one of them to please
come back to life.

3.
Horses hidden in hoarfrost
keep emerging in bad dreams.

Horses run through hoarse
barns. Hemlines narrow their slits.
You can stick a baby horse inside

a nightmare conveyor belt.
Dripping aborted debris
onto a field
unexpectedly.

Torso Chamber Orchestra

1.
Even ongoing contortionism
eventually becomes a limbo land,
but how do we know when?

How do we know anything
for sure? How do we know
if it's real or another dream state?

When does the dream become
a nightmare? How does it feel
when the contortionist begins

to break? What might lie
in between those cracks? Sate?

2.
I started maniacally writing letters to
Erik Satie, every letter ending with
is this too many questions?

Check yes, no, or maybe.
He couldn't check anything,
because he was dead, but

my dream state felt a gun living
inside his skull box head,
a gun shaped like a piano key.

Pressure on the board and then
a war dancing. Fate? Or free?

3.
The dream state started shaking
then instead of waking from it
and approaching usual synthesis,

I refused to ever wake again.
However, when I stopped moving,
I could still hear the neurons firing

and it began to sound horrific.
I felt like a giant gurgle of
limping implacable groins.

I knew the season was changing or
had changed into a maroon Ouija board
on which I had charged myself

to begin to divine
an Underworld's spring.

Grave Contortionism

From the place within you
that starts talking to you
with an unfamiliar voice
telling you

"I am your Within."

Gravitate. Grab ahold
of it like a
drink or grace.

Then watch it collide
with the neighbor's house,
the unassuming wall,
the sun as it is neither
rising
or setting.

That tree looks like a torso
hypnotized into the ground,
with one branch moving up high
and another moving low
and everything is blowing
all
at once.

I am on my knees
begging for
a new
life or at least
some leverage.

Sacrifice has made my soul too
thin and brittle and about
to break. It is time
for me to scar something.

Are you available
to come over and play?

Unhinged collisions
will fall from the sky.

The sky needs to be pulled apart
into two pieces,
one to fit in each
river down.

The river of sludgy lies.
The river of cold wet truth.
Which river will hold on
to your shimmering alabaster
thighs with stalkless barnacles?

Inside stockings live my kneecaps.
Inside my hand lies a gun
metal alloy.

Inside my heart a spasm
that points to a black hole,
a red rib cage grave marker,
a spasm of light and dark flowers.

Conjured Talisman

Every red cloud appears
to be dripping
new anomalies.
Turkish Delights
erupting out of
this witch moon.

"Which
one?"

"The mouth
swoon!"

Who turned
one whole side
of the sky
into a mutant
spinning wheel?
God
but the real
one. You

know the fish
reel? Designed to turn
dust into new buds
that will froth up,
then break down.

Cracked shells,
spines draped inside
stilettos hardening into
shimmering snakes.

Silhouettes tearing
down the sky
that has changed so much
between
last night and tonight.

Minuscule crescents.
Meniscus pirouettes
into maximus piranhas
chiming within
broken bones.

"The seeker, the seeker,"
she sparkles with twisted glee.
Weeds spring up from winter,
new ornamentation will harden
those contorted bones into new.

New shapes will save you.
A phantom deer will make it across
to the other side of the road.
Sentiment in the clearing,
waxing in the waning tail spin.

Create Your Own Rise and Fall

1.
In this dream I'm at the top
of my favorite Ferris Wheel
right before it starts

falling
down.

The stars I mean
are falling. Am I Chicken
Little? Who am I when I fall?

I was never a popular star,
but that didn't mean I couldn't
make my own modifications,
convert blades into
wings I covet.

Uncertain coverings
with things hidden in between
fingernails, cages, undersides.
Ravens rise. Uneven, then
terse, about to converge upon
the magpies and fight
for an assortment of eyes,
a root system of gray skies,
killer thighs and light
that hits them just right.

2.
How can you be direct and to the point
unless you stick a hundred different things into one
small shape and pretend that means something
that can't possibly break?

It's going to break.

It's going to fall
from the top of the Ferris Wheel
& some of it will crash down
& some of it will rise up
& some of it will create
new shapes for what used to be broken
eyeballs. Multicolored with
mutilated flowers inside.

Others have their eyes shut
so they don't explode.

We need to feel
like we are something
more.

3.
Multi-sexed and reorienting
by seizing and sizing up
any rejection
into something unsinister
and far more sisterly.

Mixed breed of colors. Colored
pencils dripping
salt and choice.
Choose your own
adventure.

Dive out of the top
before it falls.

Oh Black Swan Pie Seasoned and Sliced

An amusement park ride might kill me more
than 20 years after I thought it would.
I question the rides that I chose to get on
after I get off and my head is hurting.

It's too late now. I can't spiral myself back
in time. But what I can do? I am doing it:
reaching up with both hands until my ribs
are lifted. A swan posture or song.

Oh black swan.

Oh multicolored tiara.

When is our due date again?

I'm talking to you.
I'm asking you what
is going to emerge forth from
this cracked open womb when finally,

during the wrong season,
during the right time,
I ooze out a swarm
of apples with wings.

Floating apples, floating up,
flaked with false salts and
aimed to dive back down,
hit new spillways to be broken

like unannounced construction on
the Yellow Brick Road. How can we
die when we've made it this far?
When we've made ourselves into

a new combination of witch fusion mix,
with bubbly drinks pouring out our multi
colored tiaras like succulent new
witch fairy babes. Never stop
exploding glitter, jam.

Juliet and j/j Interview Each Other

j/j - What is the strangest or most unforeseen thing with which you have ever collaborated?

Juliet - One of the recent strangest is dead birds. I don't kill birds, but if I see a dead bird on the ground, especially a tiny baby bird fetus, it tends to inspire my poetry/art flow.

*

Juliet - Do your creative streaks ebb and flow – and when they ebb, how do you create a flow again?

j/j - I don't think my writing/projects are flow-dependent: at least not in the more usual sense that flow is coupled with ebb. I would say that in many ways, I force projects into existence. While, regularly, I try to work with breath and balancing processes in my body, I find it squelching to permit breathing room in my projects. I guess I just feel that there is a lot more dynamic energetic within me, than an ebb and flow model might allow. I instigate push. If the project is a hydrothermal cave, then it (by its nature) does not need to see the light of day; it needs to engorge on the heat and minerality of me, as I enter it, it needs to suck me down, but it does not need a contrary to it in order for it to flourish. Maybe this means that I am not always the pregnant creature pushing the offspring out, so much as I am a doula: present and planning (before even going into the drama of a birth) on getting my body all bloody due to my proximity with what it is that is already going on in there.

I think it is useful, though, to pronounce that I identify as a Shaman who actively practices convergence of disparates by way of volition. Maybe that means my body and pages are a collaborative genre, driven by guaranteed reach. Many of my recent projects' fixations with narrative came for me, from practicing volition-based projects for many years prior. A longing and a lust for content, are, believe it or not, much more challenging to approach (for me) than rhythm or form or even style (swagger) is. Volition (as with many forms of path) is wise; it makes sense that it took a while for me to be lead here.

*

j/j - I am glad you collaborate with dead birds. I have done that too, in my life. What a gift to be able to experience nearness with an entity of Earth-elemental that has just passed. This reminds me of how, at the same time that they made me feel immense pain, I was also fanatical about the relevance of funerals as a child. Here is a gift-image of one of my dear friends (made friend over a long span of collaboration time with it) for you.

How do you read (or intuit?) the relationship of body to page? For you, does the body ever become the poem?

Juliet - Thank you for your gift image. Above is one of my recent dead bird fetus photos. These visuals and the thoughts they elicited ended up inspiring their way into a poem I was working on at the time, partially based on having found out that a friend of mine had been involved in a mentally abusive relationship, culminating into physical abuse. Birds aren't humans but they are real living beings and since there are a lot of small, close-to-the-ground trees in my area, I imagine that eggs can easily be flung out of their nest by larger living beings and then the cracked out fetuses are just left on the ground to die.

About funerals, I still clearly remember the visuals of one I attended in high school. Two class mates had died in a car accident and during the pre-funeral proceedings, one of their caskets was closed and the other one was open. Both inspired lots of unsettling thoughts/feelings and my view of the open casket also inspired a poem.

About the ebb and flow, I also don't feel as if I have straightforward ebbs/flows either. I feel like I am not straightforward about anything; I am ongoing circular shapes; I will not have enough time to get it all out encircled. I'm rarely ebbing; I usually have high energy; but I have a lot of different focuses and inconsistent mood shifts. It's like I'm flowing and frothing and discharging and sometimes emitting altered currents.

For me, my body does not become a poem in and of itself, BUT feelings about my body and other bodies and body-based dynamics seem to infiltrate much of my poetic content. I tend to be overly self-deprecating about my own looks and the aging process. I am not aiming to fit into the mainstream, in terms of what's viewed as physically appealing – but I want to appeal to someone and oftentimes, I don't even know if I appeal to myself. I sometimes judge myself through other people's perceived perceptions re: my looks and other parts of me. I don't have clear cut judgments of my own. I'm not black and white or yes and no about anything. I don't feel as if anything is set in stone. I'm often shifting, but not in a purposely shifty way.

Oftentimes instead of attempting to express my mixed up viewpoints with straightforward words, I do so with poetry and visual art (like painting/collage art hybrids) and then let others interpret it how they will. I am often very uncertain about how others interpret my body and mind; likewise, I am often uncertain about how others interpret my poetry/art.

Bird fetuses, other carcasses, abandoned flesh, used flesh, abused flesh, relationship issues, body based issues, and fear of death often infiltrate my mind in one way or another - and much of my poetry and art helps me express those infiltrations rather than repress them. I love creative expression, but sometimes post-expression, I feel like my content might be overly repetitive about myself, mind/body, life/death and what is the point of it all.

*

Juliet - Do you feel that your poetry and art have more widespread points than just your own in-depth personal expression - if so, what are some of those points?

j/j - I appreciate your speaking of your uncertainty regarding aesthetics, exterior judgments and the aging process. It is good to hear how you engage the flurry/fury that embodied human form can be.

I definitely do feel that my projects involve potentially enabling widening more than they do points. While, of course, as my work is admittedly inseparable from the body (and therefore does work with/in "in-depth personal expression") it also takes responsibility for being a channel for energy that has been cleansed somehow by sonorous and/or language-force, takes psychic surgery very personally, prioritizes the subverting of social norm and cues which belittle hysteria and other forms of Priest/ess practice as valid methods for living and doing spiritual/emotional/alchemical work and works with pronouns (and identity, authenticity, embodiment, queerness and safe space) vigorously. These are subjects that are indelibly and constantly applicable. Therefore both my content and my forms fixates on them.

*

j/j - On the emission of altered currents: tell me how you work with structures in a poem or a project? Do they enable further alterations of currents? Do you see your moods (and their shifts) as inhibitors or catalysts of a poem? Or something else?

Juliet - For the most part, I'm pretty uninhibited in terms of how I express myself, TOO uninhibited by some people's standards. Too much sharing can involve risks and judgments - but if I'm going to be judged by judgmental others, they might as well judge pieces of the real me and/or what I chose to create and express, so I'll continue to express myself as I desire to.

My moods can be catalysts, but so can sound, imagery, memories, and imaginings. Past experiences and/or visual images and/or emotions often vibe with current thoughts – sometimes like a broken articulation, sometimes like an alternating current, sometimes like colorful currants.

As far as structuring my poems, I tend to have lots of individual lines written down (whenever a line emerges from me, I try to write it somewhere before it escapes), and when I sit down and concentrate on creating poetry, I sometimes slowly, sometimes quickly fuse certain lines together. I start out lying on the floor writing with my hands. Once the poem reaches a certain state of emergence, I move to the computer and type and work on line breaks, formatting, rearranging, revising…

*

Juliet - With a large poetry landscape, both online and in print, and so many varieties of content, how do you decide what poetry to read via literary magazines, books, or other sources?

j/j - I want to say, firstly, that I am sad and sorry that people have judged you/your work. I don't find judgment to be even relevant as an aspect of the poetic/page endeavor. I really do feel that there are much more creative ways to engage each other on the level of the work. We need encouragement, all of us. We need seeing. I feel that criticality in general cuts genuine awe out of the picture.

Thank you for keeping the ape-like position of pages-by-hand (probably lying on your belly) in your writing practice. I think it is important that we do these things, the things that bring our human bodies into the work. If we don't add layers to our work with a page, by way of various inclusions (the human body especially) then the whole writing/poetry realm can become strict, leveled out, solely intellectual. It can even become dogmatic and exclusive (which I feel robs from its potential).

As far as reading goes, there are really two pieces to that for me. I decided, long ago (as a result of my frustration with the bully-like tone of general criticality) that I would be open to reading and coming up with upholding and tonally encouraging methods for interacting with people's work: basically anyone's work. I believe it is possible to reach into content and from within it, via that reach, to add buoyancy. We do not have to function in the same ways for me (as a gesture of love) to support you. It feels much better for me to hold you up than it does for me to pull you down. I really do feel interaction is for address of karmic complexities and I want to work therein with kindness.

For this reason, I created a style of interaction with others' work that I all Creative Engagements. Some of these have appeared at Big Other, EOAGH and other places. So, first answer: I will read anything genuine and work to find ways to support it.

Next layer of answer: lately I have been involved in what I am calling The Mystical Sentence Projects. I love Max Valerio's memoir, doug rice's experiments rooted in wandering sentence, Anna Joy Springer's and Roxanne Carter's recent works published by Jaded Ibis. There have been writing eras in the past, in which my structural and content-based works were akin to things much different than what I am drawn to now. The work progresses by way of what has been built before. Nothing is left behind, but the flesh-tower grows with all of these tows. During the pre eras, I liked experiments with form that let data of the body flood on through: Andrew Peterson, lark fox and others. There have been a few steadfast presences, of course: Brossard, Duras, Darrieussecq. Each of these have been my friends in different ways.

*

j/j - Can you speak (to the degree that it feels right to you) to your injury and how you work with it re writing practice? Does it bleed over? Blend in? Or?

Juliet - First a few remarks on your last answers. I really appreciate your comment about judgments and I agree. I especially love your description "that criticality in general, cuts genuine awe out of the picture".

Yes about the lying on my belly - focusing on my body and my brain, my feelings and my thoughts, the writing utensil in between my fingers, my body and the pages on the floor, and the positioning/re-positioning of my body and thoughts and words and what emerges and how it FEELS.

Along the lines of your reading, I also don't have any set type of poetry that I'm more associated with than other types. There are certain poets I adore, certain poems I adore, certain literary magazines I adore, but it's a pretty vast and ongoing spectrum. Sometimes it seems like some writers consider themselves "academic" and other writers consider themselves "outsider writers" – and I'm not particularly for or against either of those realms – but the part I don't relate to is why anyone chooses to place themselves/their creative work in any one category. I very much appreciate your Creative Engagements with all kinds of writing, which potentially supports the creative process, without being mostly focused on a certain sort of finished product. Your positive and passionate approach towards all genuine creative work is admirable and awe inspiring and I feel similarly.

Regarding my injury, I think you're referring to my unexpected aneurysm/carotid artery dissection/stroke several years ago, which resulted in some brain loss and a side effect of mild aphasia. Oddly enough, the brain loss was in the area of my brain associated with words, so I was extremely worried at first – since for years, reading and writing and especially poetry had been my primary passion in life and what if my brain had lost parts of its strength associated with my primary passion?

The fact of the matter is that my passion for words, unique individual expression, poetry, and art helped me heal.

My reading and writing is still a bit slower than it used to be, but my main word issues are with easy little words rather than unique creative expression – and if I have trouble with an easy little word, I can often just explain something differently.

My brain is a little bit different than it used to be – not so much in terms of my overall personality – but in terms of being more visual than it used to be. I sometimes visualize certain things faster and more specifically than I can verbally express them.

In the last few years, in addition to writing, I also have times of focusing on visual art, especially painting/collage art hybrids – and even if I can't explain it specifically, that process (and sometimes its results) feel like a visual poem to me.

*

Juliet - How do you get your creative work out there/let other people know about it without being/feeling overly self-promotional? (This is an issue I've been wondering about in recent years, so I'm interested in your thoughts on it.)

j/j - First: good, I am glad we are nodding together in agreement regarding how detrimental it is to clear-cut awe. I mean: enough of the Earth is under attack (in various forms) already. We certainly don't need to be adding to that by attacking each other. Thank you for convening with me regarding this important ethics piece.

I enjoy hearing about the event-induced evolution of your brain and body. Aphasia is intense: a jolt or disconnect between what you feel (your desire to say) and actually saying it. What specific form(s) of aphasia did you experience? More Anomic? Or was it in the Expressive/Receptive manner?

I feel joyed (it is my hope that we can all feel this in one way or another) art/writing helped you heal. The capacity for us to be rectified, vivified, resurrected by our work with matter (that is what art/writing is, yes?) is hopeful. Matter and reach are always here for us, even when parts of our home are lost to a flood, or we or a loved one dies or we literally witness a baby bird slip out of what should be its shelter: safe space at the top of the tallest tree.

Now, onto your question: I think that I do feel overly self-promotional. I feel that I have to be okay with calling out my own accuracies and names in public if I want to be publically acknowledged in ways that reify those accuracies. I guess I am saying I am used to understanding my body as my most enabling stage: the place in which elaborate ceremonial gores are performed. For this reason, I have come to treat the promotion of my work as a type of pleasure. This is certainly a place where I can feel my own power as an agent of deep agency and frankly, in a world where many quotidian tasks do not exactly feel like pleasure, it is a gift to be able to address my work in ways that taste/feel good to me. When I was a child (raised Mormon) I was never allowed to drink tea. There was dogma attributed to why, but I simply, also, did not have access to tea. Now, I drink tea all the time. I love tea. There is a certain element of choice to it, like: though there is no rule-book that says I must drink tea or I must not drink tea (must promote my work in such and such a way or must not promote my work in a way that I can also enjoy), I drink tea because I want to. It tastes and feels good to me, and I figure if it brings me pleasure it is something I can consider mine. It is another layer of my ethics that I live to be grateful for what is mine, what I have.

*

j/j - New tone of question now: Is there a spiritual path that you follow, personally? If so, how does that path relate to your work with/identification with "gurlesque"?

Juliet - Regarding parts of your last answer, I have Anomic aphasia; I minor version compared to how severe it is for some people. I have to concentrate to get easy little words like colors, foods, names etc… Sometimes a word will come out fine; then mere minutes later, the same word won't come out. Sometimes my brain emits the first LETTER of a word and visualizes its approximate LENGTH - and then I have to concentrate hard to make the whole word emerge.

I love your description, *"the place in which elaborate ceremonial gores are performed"*. That makes sense to me in terms of some of my own poetic thoughts and expressions.

Now onto your question about my spiritual path. I was raised Catholic and at some point, my mind began to perceive Catholicism as something that was not my own choice – it seemed clichéd, fake, and forceful to me and also judgmental of me. I'm not saying that's how Catholicism is for everyone; I'm saying that is how my mind began to interpret it. As someone who does not perceive things in a black & white, right & wrong, heaven or hell sort of manner, it just didn't work for me – yet I felt like it was still being forced upon me to an extent – and so for quite a few years, I had some anti-Catholic feelings going on (they even worked their way into some of my older poetry). I spent some time researching other sorts of spirituality too, including witchcraft, but ultimately I considered myself an atheist for many years.

In more recent years, I reconsidered my thoughts/feelings about spirituality and now I feel agnostic more than atheist. I think that our bodies/minds/brains have huge power potentials – and it's hard to define those powers.

Although I don't personally relate well to standard religions, I'm open to anyways thoughts/feelings on religion or spirituality, as long as they don't try to force their viewpoint upon me, as if there's only one right way to view such things. Personally, my spiritual realm is related to my brain and how it creatively expresses. I feel spiritual about poetry and art. Even if some of my subject matter seems dark, negative, or twisted, the fact that I focused on expressing myself my way is uplifting to me – sometimes even like a higher power for me.

Again, others may choose to interpret/express/feel deeply about their own higher powers and belief systems however it works best for them and I'm willing to accept others' interpretations as long as they don't try to force it on everyone else like it's the only right way.

Adhering to one set viewpoint for everyone strikes me as close minded – and I think open minds are much more valuable and have much more potential than closed minds.

Even though Catholicism is not my spiritual path, some specific detailed perceptions/interpretation of being raised that way have found their way into past poetry of mine - and even some more recent poetry has been impacted by the horrific torture of female saints - and part of my mind perceives that as some sort of horror movie "gurlesque" fusion mix.

*

Juliet - Tell me more about your spiritual perceptions and your gender shaman-ism.

j/j - Interestingly enough (and I hope *they* feel it as an honor to them) my own spiritual perceptions and Gender Shamanism are strongly affected by saints. Female saints are vigorous progenitors of the vivid, of viscera as both place and path in which to practice and, due to that fact, I feel safe being wrapped up in them: their cloaks, the length (or shorn-quality) of their hair, the shapeliness of their visions.

I am a practicing Priest/ess (the slash is because, for *me*, provocative work with the unseen realms does not happen by way of one gender (or anything singular for that matter) but is instead very mixed). I am also a practicing Shaman. I would say that at their base, both of these signifiers (Priest/ess and Shaman) root the work in an overlap so rich that binary distinctions (light and dark, good and evil, positive and negative, uplifting and saddening) are less relevant than the alchemical momentums which reverberate from them, making deepening fusions possible. Ordinary religions can be very limiting. I am interested in perpetuating images, feelings and forms of and for the extraordinary life.

This may mean, if the base of a certain project is trying to get at, say, the power of the pineal gland, or the brazen and radical act of claiming your genitals in a self-invented context as A) your own and B) fodder by which transmogrifications or any other form of interstellar travels may occur, then I will engage page in that way. I guess I am saying the only thing I really answer to (and this is intentional) is the quality and rigor of my work ethic and the poise of pages as potentially fruitful posits. The under-guts are glamorous to me. They are what I bow to and how I bow.

More than anything else, I am compelled by the ritual moment: the height in which transfusions can occur. I avidly pursue magics of many sorts and I perceive my books as psychic surgery of psychic and physical states. My books are *ands*. For these reasons the work is, at its base, engagement of matter for the sake of_____. You stroke the wood before wrestling with it to turn it into a boat; you lay your head against the mast of the boat while your fishing line sways in the sea. This is what it is all for to me: arrange disarray, alert awry.

Saint Elisabeth of Hungary snuck loaf after loaf of bread to the poor. When she was caught and asked probingly what she was carrying, knowing she might well die at this juncture, I imagine her taking a slow breath and tilting her head toward the oncoming moonlight. Did her eyelids buzz before she opened her apron keeping her eyes closed, and in place of the loaves that would get her sentenced to some kind of horrible torture, many roses falling out?

*

j/j - You speak about a crux of your spirituality being in the artistic expression and relations with your brain. Can you tell me if there is anyone/anything that you answer to or are prostrate to in that kind of devotion?

Juliet - There is no ONE that I predominantly answer to; not that I don't pay attention to others (in some respects, I pay too much attention to others), but I try to let my primary focus exist within my own brain waves and my own creative flow and my own productivity. I am creatively attracted to positive flow extracted from negative flow and other mixes.

I like your use of the word under guts and I'm willing to explore my own guts and reveal/express them however I choose, but despite being willing to expose myself through writing and art, I won't bow down prostrate to anyone else or force myself upon anyone else.

I don't desire to control or be controlled physically or mentally. I do crave physical and mental stimulation and in-depth connection, but I am less trusting of such connections than I used to be.

*

Juliet - Is there anything else in particular you would like to express, related to and/or aside from what we have already talked about in this interview? Word-based, art-based, body-based, food-based, sound-based, or anything else.

j/j - Thank you for your honesty regarding not wanting to control or be controlled. If you feel something that clearly, it, of course, would permeate your view. I am sure your work is nourished by such clarity. I feel a bit sad re the piece of your answer that talks about how trusting you are now versus what you used to feel. I always feel this way with what I perceive to be losses. I am sorry for anything that has ever happened to you, that has hurt you, forced retraction regarding something you actually deserve.

Word-based: words are more than language to me. They are little bolts, jolts of light, symbols and systems capable of enabling. Words are ways to make little worlds in which resounding can occur. Words are matter by which to graft new forms of environment and safe space. I depend on words in so many ways. They are access to so much vibrating excess, how an intuition becomes a speaking image, a realm.

Body-based: I have synesthesia. Often sound and sight (image) exchange. There are other modalities too: color and vibration. How to articulate experience then? When I read and swallow in words, sentences, I often feel a buzzing just outside of the frame of my physical body, sort of like standing by a loud speaker as intense music blasts at a dance club.

Food-based: food has been a bit of a loaded subject for me in my life. By loaded, I mean it is charged. There were initial abuses on my body: an attempt at socializing me with body hatred. There were many different dysphorias, and there were the ways that I dealt with them via food in order to keep myself alive, to keep the knife in my hands away from my wrists.

There were many years in practice, when I worked with food in the context of asceticism. That work was about how to live as embodied fullness, when not living in fullness. Can something come from nothing? Abiogenesis says it can. You reach your hand into the void of your empty body and pull out an entire, frothing cornucopia. People marvel. Then you get asked to join the circus so others can watch you for entertainment.

There have also been very intentionally hedonistic eras of embodiment. These were not practiced as opposites to asceticism, but as ways to run my hands through flesh in a different way: fatter, juicier, the ripe peach tree miraculously growing all manner of fruits and not just peaches.

For me it is about alerting form and there are many methods by which alerting can occur. Alchemical alerting is sacred to me. It is precisely what makes my body alive (more than something, simply inherited (as a meal without meaning (on the table at childhood)) ever could be.

Spirit-based: As long as I can work with them on my own terms (as a friend in ever expanding fields) and am not forced into working with them in the context of dogma or history or linearity, I am profoundly enabled by many forms of spirituality (possibly even any form). The mystic's resin is thick within my blood and bones. I can feel it swell in the ideas, populate my dreams. To know how to work with and integrate such resin is the work. For me, that is ethics and it must be an ethics that slithers and contorts: moves alongside the moods and anarchic ministries, the manifestations of this particular minstrel.

Submission-based: I think I might in fact, want to be owned. But I don't want to be owned by just anyone. I want to be owned by the person who treats what they own as an altar: taking responsibility for its well-being. I want to rest in a non-debatable belonging. Now, I prefer to explore this yearning by way of varying forms of kink, over, say, commerciality or consumerism.

Emancipation-based: as a practicing Priest/ess and Shaman, I really enjoy working with Chöd. Known as "cutting through the ego" and then making it edible (content for the developing body to consist of) Chöd just makes sense to me. There has been intense flooding in Colorado over the last week or so. Newscasters are calling it a "once in two hundred year event." The other day, when I went to the water's edge it was obvious to me: the flood water engorging is the God/dess-to-Gaia-stratum consuming itself. This destruction is a deifying process: a curious cleansing. The crops will grow so much better in the next few years than they did this year, because of the carnal chew. Oh, there is a laugh too, and it can be read as sinister and sensuous in the exact same moment. I find myself as a way of eventually finding others, within that.

*

j/j - Do you have a favorite season and does it have poetic relevance for you?

Juliet - The Fall is my favorite season of the year. Seasons don't particularly inspire or infuse themselves into my poetry, but some seasonal temperature-based risks and spews do (such as rain, thunder, lightning, hail, tornadoes, volcanoes, magma) and the moon has inspired a few poems, especially when its color was red.

Speaking of red, I recently wrote myself a list of words that I seem to use repeatedly (maybe too repetitively) in poem after poem. This isn't purposeful; but it's something I've noticed when reading a batch of my poems in a row. Repeated word choices of mine are red, holes, dolls, borderline, poison, writhing, ripped, socket mauled, consumption, erotica, mutate, hissing, blood, bulging, thighs, tentacles and various kinds of sea creatures (especially urchins and octopus) and birds.

On a semi-related note, perhaps it's a semi-seasonal thing that bird's nests, eggs, and living and dead baby birds feel inspirational to me - especially newly born or died too soon tiny fetal size. Also pigs – especially fetal pigs available for dissection or taxidermy.

*

Juliet - Do you have a favorite holiday and/or do you create your own special days – and how do you celebrate?

j/j - For me Valentine's Day and my anniversary (coming up soon in October) are basically the same holiday. While these are no doubted my favorites I also like to treat them as models for how to act (regarding intimacy and putting forth effort in order to ensure that the dream of the Beloved in form, stay alive) in the quotidian. I would not want to stay on a planet where there was no guarantee that passionate love would be felt every day: even as the norm of days. I am a ceremonialist and a hysteric. This means the combination of profound centered-ness and feral, sound/body movement is the form and contents of celebration that most feed me. I like to know that any number of gods/goddesses/hybrids could rest easy in the shapeliness of the ceremony: the calm ones and the ones, like Kali, who need to yell and cut the heads of dark roses off by knife before eating sucking the chlorophyll from them.

Acknowledgements:

Thank you very much for the poetic support of the editors and presses in which some of these poems first appeared or are forthcoming.

"Chords", "Blood Red Cloudbursts" and "Torso Chamber Orchestra" within *Menacing Hedge*

"What Do You Desire For This Valentine's Day?", "The Pumpkin Gut Fur of the Fairy Tale", and "A Multitude of Red Ring Fingers" within *New Manifestos*

"Pre-Bacon" and "Blood Bath Through Water Balloons" within *Horse Less Review*

"Chicken Feed" within *Uppagus*

"Inside Out Again", "Elated Excavation", "Cuckoo Loincloth", "Disinfectant or Douche?," and "The Healing Potion Explodes" within *ALTPOETICS*

"Goop" and "Anti-Mold Momentum" within *Crisis Chronicles*

"Access Achieved Then Denied" and "Wonderland or Wanderlust" within *ILK*

"Clots Push Over the Edge" within *Stirring*

"Crooked Clock Work", and "Defenestration Below Ground" within *Reality Beach*

"The Secret Carnage of Female Fairies While They Wait in Women's Rooms" within *Luna Luna Magazine*

"Fugative Dive" within *Curious Specimens, a Wunderkammer Anthology*

"Animal Mutation" and "Grave Contortionism" within *Pith*

"Instead of the Doctor" within *Gargoyle*

"A Tiny Unbroken Snow Flower Stuck Inside" within *Arsenic Lobster*

"It's a Bird...It's a Plane...It's..." within *Tallow Eider*

"Misshapen Mouths" within *A-Minor*

"Testing" within *Rogue Agent*

"Below Water Whores Bemoan" and "Oh Black Swan Pie Seasoned and Sliced" within *Milkfist*

"Broken Burial" within *Ghost Proposal*

"Create Your Own Rise and Fall" within *The Fem*

The poems "Chords", "What Do You Desire For This Valentine's Day?", "Inside Out Again", "The Pumpkin Gut Fur of the Fairy Tale", "Goop", "Inside Out Entangled Twine", "Elated Excavation", "Cuckoo Loincloth", "Paradoxical Flight", "Paradoxical Dive Back Down", "Access Achieved Then Denied", "Anti-Mold Momentum", "Wonderland or Wanderlust", "Banshees", "Go Ahead and Rip Off These Witch Tits and See What Happens Next", "Clots Push Over the Edge", "Blood Red Cloudbursts", "Broken Burial", "Disinfectant or Douche?", and "The Healing Potion Explodes" also appear within the chapbook *Dive Back Down*, published by Dancing Girl Press in 2015.

Bios:

~j/j hastain is a collaborator, writer and maker of things. j/j performs ceremonial gore. Chasing and courting the animate and potentially enlivening decay that exists between seer and singer, j/j hopes to make the god/dess of stone moan and nod deeply through the waxing and waning seasons of the moon.

~Juliet Cook is a grotesque glitter witch medusa hybrid brimming with black, grey, silver, purple, and red explosions. Her poetry has appeared in a peculiar multitude of literary publications.
You can find out more at www.JulietCook.weebly.com.

www.ingramcontent.com/pod-product-compliance
Lightning Source LLC
Chambersburg PA
CBHW052026290426
44112CB00014B/2397